SURPRISING SCIENCE

Ripsticks and Scooters

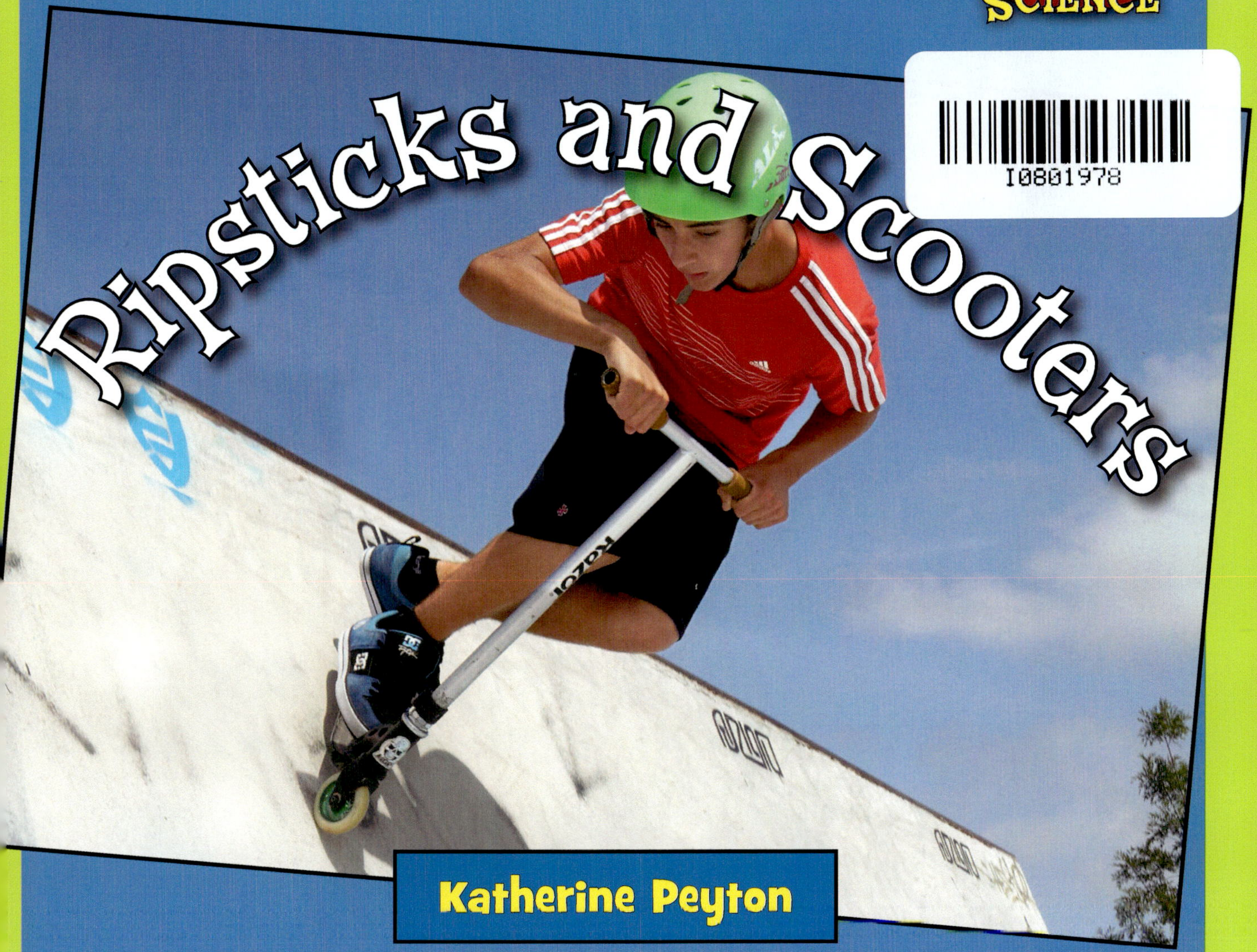

Katherine Peyton

Cavendish Square
New York

Published in 2014 by Cavendish Square Publishing, LLC
303 Park Avenue South, Suite 1247, New York, NY 10010

First Edition

CPSIA Compliance Information: Batch #WW14CSQ

All websites were available and accurate when this book was sent to press.
Library of Congress Cataloging-in-Publication Data
Peyton, Katherine.
Ripsticks and scooters / by Katherine Peyton.
p. cm. — (Surprising science)
Includes index.
ISBN 978-1-62712-316-7 (hardcover)
ISBN 978-1-62712-317-4 (paperback)
ISBN 978-1-62712-318-1 (ebook)
1. Scootering — Juvenile literature.
2. Scooters — Juvenile literature. I. Title.
GV859.77 P49 2014
796.6—dc23

Printed in the United States of America

The photographs in this book are used by permission and through the courtesy of: Cover photo by © age fotostock/Alamy; © age fotostock/Alamy, 1; © chungking/Shutterstock.com, 3; Joyradost/Ripstik1/Own work/GNU Free Documentation License, 3; © 2xSamara.com/Shutterstock.com, 4; © pio3/Shutterstock.com, 4; © sergeevspb/Shutterstock.com, 5; Thepost001/Ripstik1/Wikipedia EN/GNU Free Documentation License, 6; © Kryvenok Anastasiia/Shutterstock.com, 7; Mbdortmund/Werne-160-Skaten/Own work/GNU Free Documentation License, 8; © Monkey Business Images/Shutterstock.com, 9; © Catalin Petolea/Shutterstock.com, 10; © liubomir/Shutterstock.com, 10; © Jorg Hackemann/Shutterstock.com, 11; Dieter Clasen/Waveboard in Fahrt 1/Transferred from de.wikipedia/Creative Commons Attribution-Share Alike 2.0 Germany license, 12; Jesse Palmer/MS-130B1/Scootering_in_rain_2370572326_c00dc5449_z.jpg/Creative Commons Attribution-Share Alike 2.0 Generic license, 13; © Greogy Johnston/Shutterstock.com, 14; © Jorg Hackemann/Shutterstock.com, 14; AngryJulieMonday/Boy on electric scooter 5988226382 e289654724 z/Flickr: Angry Kid and the eSpark Razor Scooter/Creative Commons Attribution 2.0 Generic license, 15; © stockyimages/Shutterstock.com, 16; J/Razor old a/Own work/Creative Commons Attribution-Share Alike 3.0 Unported license, 16; © Rob Hainer/Shutterstock.com, 17; © bunebake/Shutterstock.com, 18; © bunebake/Shutterstock.com, 18; © bunebake/Shutterstock.com, 19; Joyradost/Ripstik2/Own work/GNU Free Documentation License, 20; © bunebake/Shutterstock.com, 21.

Editorial Director: Dean Miller
Art Director: Jeffrey Talbot

Content and Design by quadrum
www.quadrumltd.com

Scooters and Ripsticks

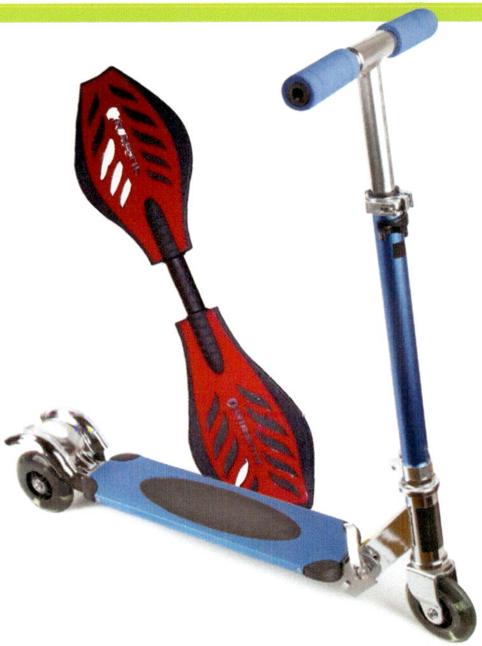

CHAPTER 1

Old scooters had four wheels like skateboards!

Rip and Scoot

Have you ever used scooters or ripsticks? Scooters have been around for at least a **century** and continue to remain popular. The latest trend, however, is a ripstick. Ripsticks seem to be taking the roller world by storm.

Three-wheeled scooters are quite popular among kids.

A scooter is also known as a push scooter or kick scooter. It is a two-wheeler with a handlebar and wheels. To move, a rider keeps one foot on the scooter and pushes with the other foot.

A ripstick is a part of the skateboard family. But a ripstick is not a skateboard; it is a type of **caster board**. This two-wheeler is similar to the scooter. It is powered by the rider pushing the ground. The main difference from a scooter is that the ripstick has no handle or support.

Scooters are fun to ride. They're not just for kids. Everyone from **toddlers** to teenagers, and even adults, can be seen on scooters. One thing that makes them great is that you can start riding them at a very early age. This is thanks to the new range of three-wheeled models that are specially made for very young kids.

On the other hand, the normal two-wheeled scooters have height adjustable handlebars, and can be made big and sturdy enough for adults, too.

The only way to stop a ripstick is by reducing your speed and jumping off!

Although it is like a modified version of the old skateboard, the ripstick is actually a caster board. Caster boards are designed by connecting two individual **pivoting** plates with a metal bar in between, known as a torsion bar. This torsion bar enables the shifting and pivoting between the two platforms. Each platform is mounted on top of a small caster wheel that can rotate 360 degrees! You can ride caster boards lots of places, such as hilly and flat surfaces, and ramps and rails, too.

Zipping around on your scooter should be as safe as it is fun. Helmets are cool; accidents are not.

CHAPTER 2

Old-school scooters were made by attaching wheels and a handlebar to a couple of old wooden boards.

Scooter and Ripstick History

Scooters were invented in Germany in 1817. They were quite popular in the 1950s, and were **trendy** off and on until the skateboards became popular during the 1980s. The 90s revolutionized the scooter. In 1990, Swiss inventor Wim Ouboter perfected his new designs and invented the modern kick scooters that we see today. A sleeker **micro** scooter arrived on the scene, which was made of **aluminum**. It had a narrow **deck** and small **polyurethane** wheels.

Let's get to know the story behind ripsticks. Caster boards were initially a mix of the skateboard and snowboard. Even though the Wave Board was the first caster board in the market, it was the ripstick that made caster boarding popular.

The first ripstick was called the Classic. It became a very popular product in 2007. The ripstick is now available in several different models such as the RipStik G, the Air Pro, and the Ripster.

People all around the world use scooters. In the 1990s, the scooter became a popular way to travel in Japan. In Germany, nurses used scooters to whip down long hospital hallways!

CHAPTER 3

The new lightweight folding scooter has inspired a sport called freestyle scootering.

Types of Scooters

There are many companies that produce different types of scooters today. They come in various different sizes, designs, and colors, too!

Many kids start with the basic three-wheeled versions, such as the mini scooter, and progress to JD Bugs and Razors. The toughest ones to handle are the top-of-the-range stunt scooters that you may see in skate parks as riders perform various tricks.

Some scooters have mini motors which make them easier to ride!

The design of the scooter has not changed a great deal since it was invented. It still has a platform with either one or two wheels at the front to control its **steering** and one or two wheels at the back, depending on whether it is a **trike** or a scooter. One major difference that has changed over the years is the material used in making a scooter. Children's scooters are usually made using lightweight aluminum instead of wood. They also have a folding **mechanism** that makes it easier to carry them around and store safely.

The Razor scooter uses strong aluminum that can easily support up to 1100 pounds!

CHAPTER 4

It is advised that nobody weighing more than 220 pounds should ride a ripstick.

Rapid Ripsticks

The ripstick is unlike any scooter or skateboard! Unlike a normal skateboard, you don't need an initial kick or push to start moving on a ripstick. Instead, you can just twist back and forth to get moving!

A ripstick has only two wheels. Where you place your feet on a ripstick is very important. You need to step on the boards so that one wheel is directly underneath each foot. The weight of your body pressing down on the wheels helps you keep your balance. If you do not keep your feet right above the wheels, you might fall off your ripstick!

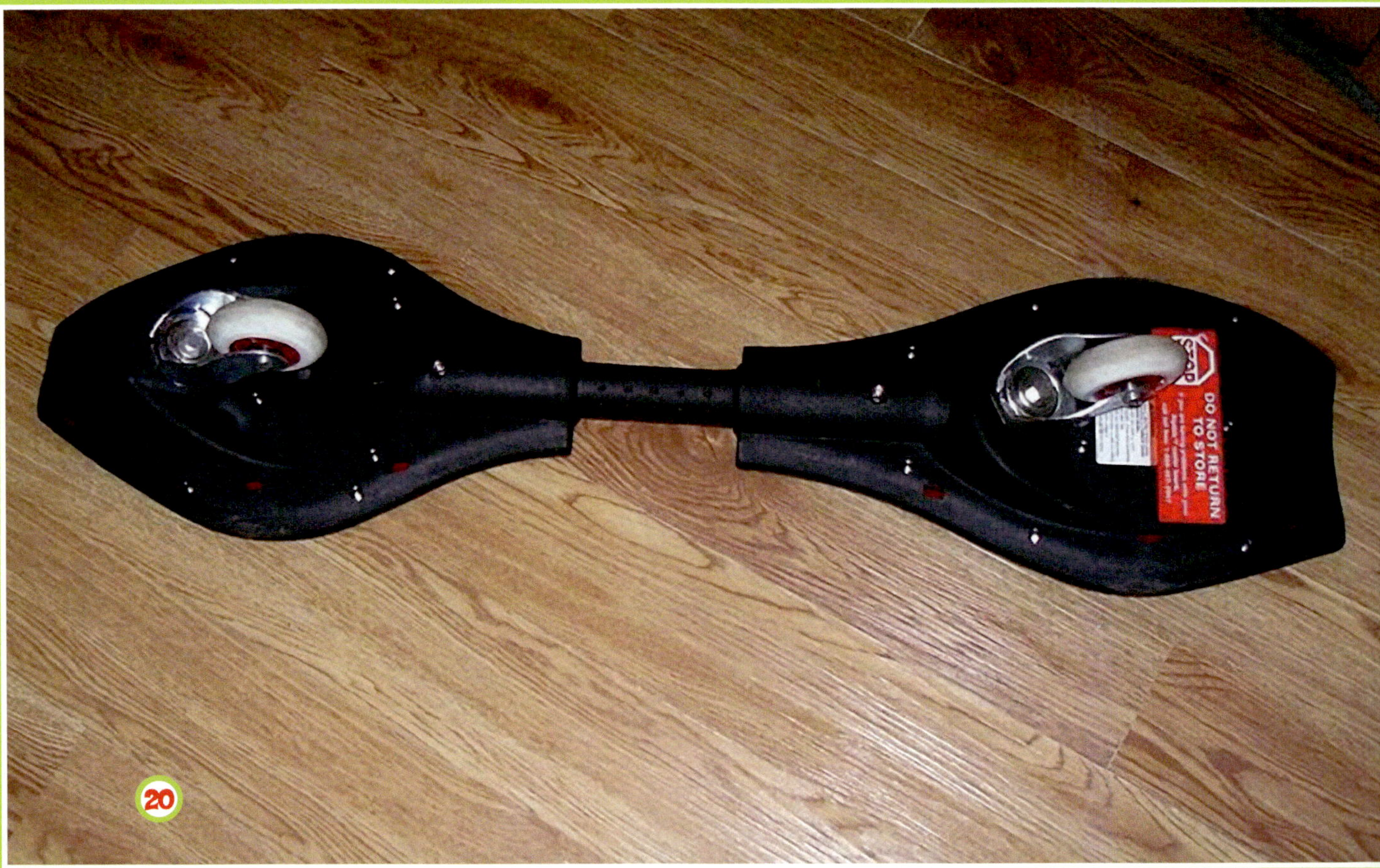

To turn the board, you must twist it. The front and back platforms tilt independently, making it possible to turn the board to point in a new direction. You can have a lot of fun with a ripstick or a scooter. They can be useful vehicles to help you get around or cool toys that help you do tricks.

There are several models of ripsticks - the Classic, the Air Pro, the RipStik G, and the Ripster.

Glossary

aluminum [ah-LOO-mi-num] a versatile metal

caster board [KAST-er BORD] a two-wheeled board

century [SENT-shu-ree] a span of one hundred years

deck [DECK] the base boards or planks of a scooter

mechanism [MEK-ah-ni-zim] a technical system of machinery

micro [MY-crow] smaller than average

pivoting [PIV-uh-ting] a rod on which another part rotates or swings

polyurethane [po-lee-UR-eth-ane] a synthetic material, similar to plastic

steering [STEER-ing] a mechanism used to turn a vehicle

toddlers [TOD-lurz] children between the ages of one and three

trendy [TREN-dee] fashionable

trike [TYRKE] a three-wheeler vehicle

Books to Discover

Case, Jeremy. *Scooters!: The Ultimate Guide to the Coolest Ride.* London: Aladdin Publications, 2001.

Rosenberg, Aaron. *Kick Scooters: Techniques and Tricks.* New York: Rosen Publishing Group, 2003.

Goodfellow, Evan. *Street Skateboarding: Flip Tricks.* Chula Vista, CA: Tracks Publishing, 2005.

Websites to Explore

eHow - Types of Ripsticks
http://www.ehow.com/list_6801053_ripstick-types.html

eHow - How to Choose a Kick Scooter
http://www.ehow.com/how_18564_choose-kick-scooter.html

Index